Benedict Arnold

by Timothy S. Corbett

✒ P9-BBN-463

HOUGHTON MIFFLIN HARCOURT
School Publishers

PHOTOGRAPHY CREDITS: **Cover** The Granger Collection, New York. **Title Page** © North Wind Picture Archives. **3** The Granger Collection, New York. **4** The New York Public Library/Art Resource, NY. **5** The Granger Collection, New York. **6** Hulton Archive/Getty Images. **8** © Christie's Images/SuperStock, Inc. **9** The Granger Collection, New York. **10** © North Wind Picture Archives. **11** © Collection of the New-York Historical Society, USA/The Bridgeman Art Library. **12** © North Wind Picture Archives. **13** ©Mary Evans Picture Library/Grosvenor Prints/The Image Works.

Printed in China

ISBN-13: 978-0-547-02555-1
ISBN-10: 0-547-02555-6

11 12 13 14 0940 19 18 17 16
4500569761

Introduction

On a dark night in September 1780, General Benedict Arnold hid in the trees along New York's Hudson River near West Point. Arnold was famous as one of the best fighting generals in the entire American army. George Washington had just given him the command of the fort at West Point.

Soon, a boat carrying four men came ashore. One man stepped out of the boat and greeted Arnold. The man was an officer in the British army, Major John André.

Benedict Arnold commanded the American fort at West Point, New York.

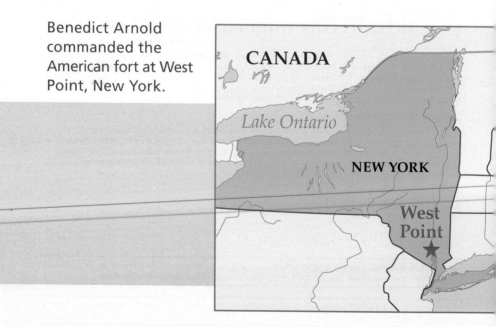

CANADA

Lake Ontario

NEW YORK

West Point

The two men should have been enemies. But beside that quiet, rural riverbank, they huddled secretively in the darkness. They were making plans. Arnold had decided to betray the American cause. He planned to surrender the fort at West Point and its three thousand American

Benedict Arnold

soldiers to the British. Taking over the fort would enable the British to control the entire Hudson River valley. The British also controlled much of the land in the southern colonies. So, this change could lead to the British winning the Revolutionary War.

Many people have wondered why Benedict Arnold became a traitor. He was a military hero. More than once, Arnold's bravery in battle had saved the American war effort. What changed him?

∞

The Young Arnold

Benedict Arnold's family had been in America for many years. His great-grandfather, the first Benedict Arnold, had been governor of Rhode Island. His mother, too, belonged to an important colonial family. But Arnold's father lost most of the family's fortune and its good name. Because his family suddenly lacked money, Benedict had to leave school at the age of 14. He returned to the family home in Norwich, Connecticut. In colonial days, a family's honor and good name were important. They could mean the difference between success and failure throughout life. Young Arnold felt shamed by his father's ruin. He vowed to regain his family's wealth and honor.

Benedict Arnold's house in New Haven, Connecticut, where he moved at age 21.

4

Unable to complete his education, Benedict needed to work for a living. His mother asked her relatives to help him learn a trade. They welcomed him into their business selling medicines. Young Benedict proved to be a good businessman. At the age of 21, he moved to New Haven. There, he began building his fortune as a merchant.

American colonists protested the Stamp Act by burning paper goods.

Arnold's business was doing well in 1765, when the British Parliament passed the Stamp Act. Many colonists began to resist these British taxes. Not everyone wanted to break with Britain. But Benedict Arnold did. He personally believed that British taxes hurt merchants and insulted the colonies.

Ethan Allen and his militia joined Arnold to attack Fort Ticonderoga.

In April 1775, news of battles at Lexington and Concord reached Connecticut. The Revolutionary War had begun. As the captain of the New Haven militia, Arnold led his soldiers toward Massachusetts. On the way, he heard that American troops lacked cannons. Arnold knew the British had cannons at Fort Ticonderoga in New York. He persuaded leaders in Massachusetts to let him organize a force to capture Fort Ticonderoga. Arnold was promoted to colonel. He joined other Patriot forces, including Ethan Allen and his militia. Together, they attacked Fort Ticonderoga. In May, they captured the fort.

Arnold felt he deserved more credit for capturing Fort Ticonderoga and its cannons. But the Massachusetts leaders questioned some of his actions. They turned down his plan to invade Canada. Disappointed, Arnold resigned from the militia. He returned home to Connecticut.

Then that fall, things changed. Arnold returned to Massachusetts. Two important American generals—Philip Schuyler and George Washington—supported Arnold's plan to attack the British in

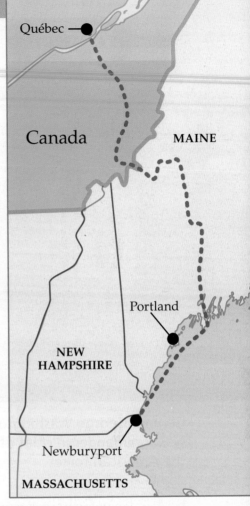

Arnold led his men along this route to Québec.

Québec, Canada. Arnold led about one thousand men through the wilderness toward Canada. His troops did not capture Québec. Yet Arnold's bravery drew wide praise, and he was promoted.

General George Washington was commander in chief of the American forces.

By 1777, Benedict Arnold was a general. Still, he did not feel appreciated. Other generals were promoted to higher ranks. Arnold believed those generals were weak and that he should have been promoted instead.

Arnold tried to resign from the army. General Washington persuaded him to stay. Washington admired Arnold's battle skills. He considered him to be his best fighting general. Washington needed Arnold for the future fighting near Saratoga, New York, in the Hudson River valley. He knew that if the British seized all of the Hudson River, the Revolutionary War might be lost.

The First Battle of Saratoga took place on September 19, 1777. Arnold led a fierce attack against the British. He urged his commander, General Horatio Gates, to launch a second attack. Gates refused, and the two men quarreled. Gates removed Arnold from command.

Arnold refused to quit. In the Second Battle of Saratoga on October 7, he disobeyed Gates's orders. Amid the peal of cannon fire, Arnold led a charge to rally the American troops. Though he was wounded, his daring leadership forced a British retreat. Ten days later, the British general surrendered. Partly due to Arnold's actions, the Battle of Saratoga was a major turning point in the Revolutionary War.

General Arnold lost his horse and was wounded at the Second Battle of Saratoga.

Many people called Benedict Arnold a hero. But the Continental Congress gave General Gates credit for Saratoga. Arnold thought that they were ignoring his contributions. Again, Arnold tried to resign, but in 1778, Washington made him military commander of Philadelphia.

Arnold's wife, Peggy, and one of their children

In Philadelphia, Arnold became friends with Americans who were still loyal to the British king. In 1779, he married Peggy Shippen. She was one of these Loyalists. Arnold's actions angered Patriots, who became suspicious. Faced with a military trial, Arnold resigned. He then secretly contacted the British in New York.

Most charges against Arnold were eventually dropped. He received official, though gentle, words of disapproval from General Washington. Arnold asked for, and received from Washington, the command of West Point. The stage was set for his stunning act of treason.

Benedict Arnold, Traitor

What led an American hero to turn on the cause for which he had fought so hard?

Historians disagree. Some say that Arnold's loyalty was to himself first. The cause came second. Others say that he grew bitter because American leaders never gave him proper credit for his military successes. It is strange, though, that a man who set out to restore his family's name ended up making that name a synonym for "traitor."

West Point looks out over the Hudson River.

What historians *do* know is that Arnold met with Major André. Then the British officer started back to his ship. When the Patriots began firing at the ship, André decided to escape overland to New York City. He never made it. The Patriots captured him. In his stockings, they found drawings of West Point and a pass signed by Benedict Arnold.

Learning that his plot was discovered, Arnold escaped. He received a large sum of money from the British and became a brigadier general in their army. Arnold fought against the Americans in Virginia and Connecticut. He died in London, England, in 1801.

Benedict Arnold fled capture at West Point.

Benedict Arnold's Life

1741   Born in Norwich, Connecticut

1755   Forced to leave school

1762   Moves to New Haven and becomes a successful merchant

1775   Takes his New Haven militia to Massachusetts
Captures Fort Ticonderoga
Leads his men to Québec

1776   Promoted to brigadier general

1777   Fights heroically at Saratoga, defies orders, and is wounded

1778   Named military commander of Philadelphia

1779   Marries Peggy Shippen

1780   Betrays the American Revolution

1780–
1781   Fights for Britain against the Americans

1801   Dies in London

Responding

✔ **TARGET SKILL** **Compare and Contrast**

Think about Benedict Arnold and Horatio Gates.
How were they alike and how were they different?
Copy and complete the diagram below.

Benedict Arnold Both   Horatio Gates

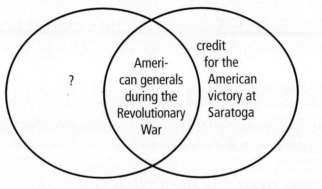

?

American generals during the Revolutionary War

credit for the American victory at Saratoga

Write About It

Text to Text Benedict Arnold decided to change
sides in the Revolutionary War. Think of another
person you have read about who changes his or her
mind about something important. Write a paragraph
explaining that person's decision.

✔ **TARGET SKILL** **Compare and Contrast** Examine how two or more details or ideas are alike and different.

✔ **TARGET STRATEGY** **Monitor/Clarify** As you read, notice what isn't making sense. Find ways to figure out the parts that are confusing.

GENRE **Narrative Nonfiction** gives factual information by telling a true story.